T0326859

THE HOURGLASS HEART

New Issues Poetry & Prose

Editor   Herbert Scott

Copy Editors   Eric Hansen, Jonathan Pugh

Readers   Kirsten Hemmy, Adela Najarro,
                              Margaret von Steinen, Cody Todd

Assistants to the Editor   Rebecca Beech, Lynnea Page,
                              Marianne E. Swierenga

Business Manager   Michele McLaughlin

Fiscal Officer   Marilyn Rowe

New Issues Poetry & Prose
The College of Arts and Sciences
Western Michigan University
Kalamazoo, MI 49008

An Inland Seas Poetry Book

 Inland Seas poetry books are supported by a grant from
The Michigan Council for Arts and Cultural Affairs.

Copyright © 2003 by Gail Martin. All rights reserved.
Printed in the United States of America.

First Edition, 2003.

ISBN   1-930974-34-5 (paperbound)

Library of Congress Cataloging-in-Publication Data:
Martin, Gail
The Hourglass Heart/Gail Martin
Library of Congress Control Number: 2003104653

Art Director   Tricia Hennessy
Designer   Carrie Durante
Production Manager   Paul Sizer
                              The Design Center, Department of Art
                              College of Fine Arts
                              Western Michigan University

THE HOURGLASS HEART

GAIL MARTIN

New Issues

WESTERN MICHIGAN UNIVERSITY

to Sarah, Bailey and Katy
to George

Contents

Three

Four

Envoi

Foreword

If the landscape of Gail Martin's poems is a *domestic* one, then it is Emily
Dickinson's wild domesticity, where innocuous-looking teapots contain
tempests, where lemons stacked in a white bowl imply grief. If these are the
poems of a mother, of a wife—which they are—then they make the claim that
motherdom, wifedom, is the kingdom of God. God scrubs the tub, carpools,
vacuums the swimming pool in her bikini. And just when we think God's got it
a tad too easy, she discovers a dead possum at the bottom of the pool. "Even
now," this woman-God sighs, "the dead can't rise without her help." Framed
thusly, sometimes tongue in cheek, sometimes sharp with the citrus of grief,
the domestic cosmology of these poems becomes holy—or apocalyptic. When
the other shoe drops, as it does in one poem in this collection, it's a "satin
spike, black, sharp / as the stakes holding a burning circus tent in place." A
woman's shoe, so "commanding" that when it falls "the whole world shifts."

This shift appears on the human scale as well. The marriage Martin
describes in her poem "Marriage" is one which "rested on small things /
collected in a reliable fashion; leaves / before snow, recyclables a day late
following / holidays." This we know; with this, we're comfortable. But the poem
takes a turn as its speaker lands upon the image of the teeter-totter, whose
balance is not "even steven . . . like balancing a budget." In fact, "A trusted
partner might back off / the low end, leaving the other to crash to the ground."
Then she zeroes in, owns it: "It happened to me once; my ankles folded and
were trapped / beneath the weight;"—and here comes the danger—"the screw
drove straight for the bone." The recess toy is all grown up, as is this speaker,
disavowed of her illusions. It's this willingness to follow an "innocent" image
to its honest, uncomfortable, even profane conclusion that gives Martin's
poems their edgy wisdom. Teeter-totters, and marriages, can screw us;
thermometers, "broken in our junk drawer," can set "mercury on the loose . . ."
ready to "contaminate the world," not unlike the dropped satin spike. And, in
"A Random Shot," Martin's speaker tells us that what lurks beneath the skin,
waiting to be revealed, is random—"the cyst on my left ovary," perhaps, or
a talent for glass blowing. "And in some of us, the gift and the whammy
are sewn into one skin." Which leads us to the third, and most harrowing,
section in the book.

We learn in this section that daughters, like lemons, can resemble grief, like thermometers can contain their own quicksilver poison. As Martin maps the months when her speaker's "daughter lost her native tongue," we find huge drifts of maternal sadness intensified by the restraint of their poetic frames. The mother-speaker's tonal shift—no carpooling Gods here—brings a new, devastating beauty to this collection. "Sometimes I think it will be like that," Martin writes, "drifts of loss, whole hills / of sorrow, me with no shovel, no strong back to tunnel out." Grief is no longer confined to the clean, white bowl—it falls everywhere; perhaps it will never stop. The nebulous drifts are defined by image patterns drawn from realms far beyond those of endangered daughters. The art of de Heem, Peeters and Beert, what they "chose to reveal, where they held back." The painful grinding of the lapidary, who works to turn suffering into story, "to smooth this / into a diagnosis we can all live with." Scrimshaw, the mother's spine itself "a totem pole carved / image by hard image," "a diorama of battle into a plum pit," a woman scratched onto a whale's tooth. The woman-God is sacrificed to her daughter's suffering. Something fiercer, toothed, Demeter-like, emerges: "Bring me antlers / shed in a February meadow—I'll show you carving."

The fourth section moves us toward something like healing, but thank God, not toward redemption or melodrama. In "Sweeping at the End of Summer," the speaker observes a woman and her broom, "left to right, left, right . . . just the sweeping." It's a quiet poem; in fact, she comments that the noise of sweeping is "so repetitive [it] feels like silence." What she comes to is an image that skillfully holds the mournful beauty which might come to us at the end of summer—"light suddenly falling short / of the window where she's seen it / each morning all summer, a branch / of dogwood turning scarlet overnight."

It is significant that we find images associated with glass blowing, its fragile intensity, throughout these poems. Martin gives us the image of the woman's heart, a hand-blown hourglass "riddled with seeds and tears" which nonetheless is strong enough to funnel "the sadness of children, the silence / of living rooms," empty, yet singing. Transmogrified once again, in "Any God," another daughter poem, the woman's heart becomes the woman's *god* (small "g," uncapitalized)—"This girl—the gift we recognize—found / and rocked, o hourglass god, beneath my heart." The tableau here seems as it should be— heart intact, daughter nested beneath it, and god, shaped like a woman, flawed, delicate, and beautiful.

—Diane Seuss

Acknowledgments

Poems in this book have previously appeared in:

Folio: "*God Uses a Power Drill,*" "*God's Turn to Carpool,*" "*God Makes Lunch*"

New Poems from the Third Coast: An Anthology of Michigan Poets: "Woman of Water," "Woman of Wood"

Poetry Northwest: "Loosestrife" (published as "Symptoms") "Marriage"

Primavera: "A Random Shot"

Rattle: "For My Mother, Afraid of the Water"

Sonora Review: "Beckon Road"

The MacGuffin: "The Trouble With Three," "Orchidelirium," "Watching the Lake Freeze Over," "Anniversaries"

The Sun: "Lemons"

"The Trouble With Three" was judged the winning poem by Alice Fulton in the 1999 National Poet Hunt sponsored by *The MacGuffin.*

One

The Trouble With Three

The woman with
three left-handed daughters
always dreams in threes:

   three bones carried
   above her head
   as she wades,

   toasters lined up
   train-fashion—engine,
   coal car, caboose,

   three blue diamonds
   excised from the eye
   of the baby,

   the painting of a dog
   with three legs she keeps
   in her refrigerator.

Pythagoras called it the perfect number.
The size of synergy, the union of body,
mind and spirit, holy trinity.

She sees the problems with it.
It's not enough for seasons, won't divide
fairly so of course there'll be howling

and bitchslapping. One always
sits in the back of the van, unbalances
the table, making you choose

which side you'll sit on. Three
offers up its middle, soft dogbelly
to be stroked, but unlike the dog,

there's always shame
attached to need, and hunger
finds itself re-labeled greed.

Very few learn to see
with the third eye,
paint that third breast,

survive with a three-chambered
heart or its metaphor, the hourglass.
Still, it's less awkward than one chopstick,

and there were times three
almost felt like an even number.
Your husband, you and the new baby.

And later, three kids in yellow pajamas
beside a Christmas tree, three frowsy peonies
in a green vase—though with peonies,
one always wants more.

Anniversaries

Every square on the calendar
is the anniversary of something.
Today my grandmother would
have been 96. Next Thursday
she'll have been dead 4 years.
May 8 might have been the day
the freak ice storm froze
peony buds like the hard knots
on a girl's chest. Or the day
a particular foreign
correspondent was found floating
in the Aegean, bullet hole
above his left eye (1948).
It is the day you threw the shoe
at your father or the second day
of your honeymoon when
you cried through New Hampshire
realizing you'd lost his name.
It is the day you failed the vision
test, made no sense of the signs.
The day after the day your
mammogram came back bad
and your breasts filled up with gravel.
It's either the day your husband
forgot to call or the day you painted
your bedroom yellow.
The day you gave up meat.
The test found you pregnant.
King Leopold decided
to lop off the hands of the men
harvesting rubber too slowly.
The day the possum drowned
in your swimming pool. You set
your hand down on a hornet's

nest. (To the hornet it was the day
the roof caved in.)
The morning you spent puking
in a hotel in Hong Kong, including
the rice and small piece of mild fish
the doctor recommended.
It could either be the day you
sat on the railroad tracks
or the day you decided to leave.
Who can name the day
7 monks immolated themselves
in front of a monastery in Burma?
The last time your child was light enough
to jump off the stairs into your arms?

Lemons

Today the bass booming
through the neighborhood is sad,
like the nuisance rose that comes back wilder

with each harsh pruning. One day
I will rip it out altogether, wearing leather gloves
to the elbow. I want to cry at all of it: the energy

of the newlyweds next door, their confidence
tackling lawn grubs, the zeal of their decorating, their fights.
How shiny black their grill. And the German shepherd

pup, ears and nose too long for who he is today,
and the bravado of the girl spray-painting
her flip-flops gold for the prom, the knees

of the mailman, still white in April, exposed
below the regulation bermudas.
I am not talking remembrances here, nor ruin.

This is not the loneliness of my grandmother's elephant
brooch, red, white, and blue rhinestones resting in my jewelry box, not
the cousin who ate candles the last three days he was alive.

It is not even a longing for the reliable fathers
in the old neighborhood, that insistent piano note
backed by strings. Today I tear up seeing vinegar

and oil refuse to mix, watching the bastard
across the street repaint the little Amish buggy
and figurines and set them for summer

on his unused porch, his tulips lined up singly,
sousaphone players in a high school band.
Today the lawnmower starts and the newspaper slaps

the front door. I see the pantry shelves crowded
with canned soup and peaches, how
lemons stacked in a white bowl resemble grief.

Woman of Pearl

At harvest, the divers come,
Japanese women trained
from childhood. Like so many
angels, they float down,
long-sleeved white cotton dresses
covering them from throat
to knee. They believe white
wards off sharks. The only
precious gem created by a living
creature, adversity forms me:
a piece of broken shell, some
tiny parasite, a grain of sand.
Call me baroque, button or blister,
my luster comes from below
the surface, light broken
up by layers of me.

For My Mother, Afraid of the Water

For the cottage, I gave you a painting of children
in bathing suits, sunning on a dock; you said
they look dead. Later, as I hauled myself dripping
onto our dock, you said with the smallest bead
of bitterness, *If I could swim like you, I'd enjoy
the lake*. Mother. You've had your whole life
to learn to swim and while it's hard to dive
down when you've been cautioned against
breaking your neck, hard to crawl with confidence
when you're thinking *clam shells rimmed with razor,
sea lampreys sizzling on trout, spinning rotors
just above*, you gave up without a splash.

You didn't have to jump or plunge, no layout, tuck
or pike from the notches cut into cliffs, no swallow dive
from the top of the waterfall. You didn't have to do it
at night. Entering the water gracefully was never
important, and diving is showy, acrobatic even when water
is a safe place to land. It was never necessary to swim
the Hellespont, be carried like Jack London, drunk, through
the currents of San Francisco Bay, drifting fast past
Solano Wharf, spurning rescuers and lights.
It wasn't necessary to hold your breath, or pull yourself along
the bottom with one finger, not necessary to know
that it was the Americans who speeded up the flutter kick, 6 beats
per arm stroke, fast feet, sloooow arms, fast feet, sloooow arms.

It's true that humans are not natural swimmers, that we must learn
from watching animals who swim by instinct, must learn
to lay our soft bodies back onto water, trust that it will hold us.
You wanted me to swim, signed me up at the old Y, read
me *Cat in the Hat* in the high-windowed lobby. Remember
the fish out of water?   And all that I should have loathed:
the toe inspections, droopy suits color-coded by ability, tied on

with shoe strings, trembling on smelly tiles practicing
elementary backstroke over and over, the appalling hook
extended to the floundering—all of this I loved.

And so today I am a flashlight fish, glowing pouches
beneath my eyes blinking on and off like the headlights
of Dad's Buick. My goggles are from the polished
clear shell of tortoise. And if they fog up, if they blur
the opposite bank, if my fingers shrivel and hamstrings pop, still
there is the stroking, the breathing, that tough rhythm.
And if some days I spit out greenbottle flies and earwigs
and if some days I swim side stroke to keep from looking
down, you wanted me to swim, so I do.

A Random Shot

When the ultrasound exposed the cyst on my left ovary
I thought about what I heard on NPR: the man who'd learned

there was a bullet in his brain. He recalled passing out after a loud ba
years earlier, assumed the blood on his head was from his fall;

his brain leaked no clues. (My doctor brother claims if you think
you're healthy, you just haven't had enough tests.) I try to picture

the cyst: a fifty-cent piece, a barnacle, a tiny helmeted passenger
assuming these eggs are still shooting the rapids.

We don't want all potentials realized. Cancers, for example.
An aptitude for argument mandating law school. I carry

the genes of a man who covers the glass of water on his bedstand
each night with a piece of paper. What he believes he prevents

is the chance of swallowing something he can't see in the dark,
a heavy-bottomed spider pulled in by gravity, the kind you wear

gloves to kill. This tendency is latent in me, like alcoholism
holed up in a dry county in Utah. We have shadowy notions

of what we carry inside, an X-ray of that brain-lodged bullet
we slap up on the viewbox to read. Sometimes we imagine

aneurysms about to blow, or clots like tiny chips of Ivory soap
damming clear veins. Less often we maintain faith

in our genes, our unclaimed talents, glass blowing maybe,
isolating radium. We don't know what we don't know.

And, in some of us, the gift and the whammy are sewn in one skin.
My artist daughter draws botanical sketches of twining peas

and primroses in black ink, paints a watercolor
of a pounding heart. Her own heart's a hand-blown hourglass,

two chambers doling out sand with each beat. She's out there
playing *guess and check*, pitching the horseshoes of fortune

like the rest of us, but she feeds two tan dogs, Bullet and Trigger,
and she cannot, for the life of her, tell them apart.

Soft Science

What Angstrom unit of sacrifice is required
of a person in a family of five? What index
counts the green seconds between when you
have time to stop the slap and opt not to?
On what scale do we rank the texture
of piano notes—C♯ is to sand what B♭
is to river, the status of shame to love?

In this marriage, the days of the week have shapes,
all rectangular except Saturday, wider at the base.
Red will always smell like chili sauce that begins
with 30 ripe tomatoes and 12 apples, a man running
a penknife beneath his fingernails. We drop to our knees
each night, secure that only ratios offer a zero point
both meaningful and absolute. We learn to detect

relationships between variables, empirical
reference points, like sad children in mirrors
needing more time to reflect. Let random errors
cancel themselves out in the long run. When mistakes
pile up like dirty snow, burying degrees of love, it's hard
to see if the variable's dependent or ready to walk alone.
How high must you raise an eyebrow, how long

must you think about frowning before the child
gets the message passed down seven generations?
Through it all, we want the kind of probability
that comes with confidence: where we steam up the windows
of the station wagon singing, where the ball whispers
sweetly through the hoop again and again and girls
with flared skirts leap onto strong backs and ride.

How complex is the computation that weighs
the impact of one saxophone on a man's heart
in Guam? How far can blue shadows extend

from broken trees this last day of January?
No score can assess the relationship of wounded
to healed, rowboat to knife to woman. How far
can fishline travel? What equation shows the progression
from pearl millet to sparrow, peanut heart to wren?

God Scrubs the Tub

God counts the rings
around the tub, numbering our baths
like the hairs of our heads. God likes
the pure grit she shakes onto her sponge.
She scours the far corner, bangs her head
on the faucet and sees stars.
The fingernails on her convincing hands
bleach white as the new moon.

God's Turn to Carpool

God parks her Cadillac a block away
so as not to outshine the yellow
school buses and Dodge Caravans
which also wait. She files her nails,
listens to *All Things Considered*, and watches
the children come toward the light.
The one with pokey lips
and the largest backpack climbs
into the backseat, settles her bottom
on the plush red interior. She breaks
God's heart. God floors it.

God Vacuums the Pool

The carpenter bangs long nails
into the sweet wood of the deck
while God vacuums the pool in her bikini.
She is watching the tendons
of his forearms glisten in the sun.
A good idea, muscles, she thinks.
She sees it on the bottom then,

wonders if it's *playing* possum.
In her infinite wisdom, knows better.
As with all death, better gone than going,
she thinks. God knows had she arrived earlier,
seen him circling, she'd have been bound
to save him. She sighs. Even now
the dead can't rise without her help.

God Packs Lunches

God spins the peanut butter thin
as silk onto the dense bread, covers
each pore so the Smucker's red
can't penetrate. When she comes to the end
of the loaf she turns the last piece facing
in. You won't even notice it's a heel.

God Uses a Power Drill

God holds the power
drill in two hands
for the first time,
and it is good.
The smell of the wood
beginning to heat up.
The controlled give
as the bit moves deeper.
She scouts around
for more things to drill,
in love with the orange
extension cord.

God and the Catamaran

God only sails the catamaran
when it's storming. She likes it fast,
hanging out there, harnessed
above it all. Hiked up on one
slicing sponson, she parts the water.
She's lost her most expensive sunglasses.
Her hair dries wild.
She can trim the sail, adjust the wind.
Her red toenails please her, braced
against the mast.

Orchidelirium

*I really have to watch myself, especially around plants.
It's like I can't just have something—I have to have it
and learn about it and grow it and master it and have
a million of it.*
            —John Larouch, convicted orchid poacher

1.
You come to see the plants, nests of hot orchids
blooming in the crotches of trees, to touch
one petal—pouch or lip—to name your nature:
Clamshell, Lonely Angel, Cherry Canary,
the moth orchids, monkey and cradle,
Frog Princess, Vesuvius, Reunion,
those few that grow completely underground—
Masdevallia, Ray Millard, Albino Green—proving
what impressed Darwin the most, their ability to adapt
almost perfectly to any environment at all.
You come to classify, crossbreed, mutate and steal
what's endangered. Orchid seeds are so light, so like dust,
that they require neither hair nor wings to stay afloat.

2.
Much here is not orchid.
Insects and water moccasins
are a given. That Crocodilians can go
a year without a meal doesn't mean
they choose to. Their appetites
will be honored, as are those of the centipedes
and mosquitoes which scout the damp openings
of my body. And even savage
needs seem poignant as I surrender
to the swamp. Touching to know
that all the cancer cell means to do,
leaving, say, a kidney to become
a fleck or shadow on a lung, is to build

another kidney. We can only try
not to trample new hybrids—*Little Songbird*—
on our craven search. Abundance
or excess—the fretting hum of low country,
the sinking into mudstink deep
with ancient livings and dyings.
No solid ground in this place, still grace.

3.
Culpable for orchid-related intemperance
in the past, I may not lie down with you.
May not bring a primrose to your yellow house
nor drink a toast to orchid fever. You offer
a book to teach me the names of the plants
in this steamy swamp, refuse to wade with me
into peculiar longing, a swelter of possibility
where I risk all for turtles, old mirrors and Ice Age fossils.
We won't travel together and oh, I understand that, respect
the complicated reasons, the variables—
the amount of wind, how much rain, which side
of the tree you cling to, whether the roots
can also be leaves. Whether the blossoms
resemble fairy or frog. Still, I'm in up to my heart.
Where there's great hunger, greed blooms.
Those who traffic in wild things carry white pillowcases, slip
between ghost orchids into the keening foliage.

Woman of Wood

Kindling so delicate
your heart cracks open
as you gather it
into your arms.
Georgia fatwood, shiny
and dry, panting for flame, ready
to give it all up to smoke. Finally,
the seasoned log of apple,
lady's scent. Can you see
my eyes in flame?
Over time, I've been felled,
bucked, skidded and hauled.
Sorted and graded by men
with big appetites, split
up the middle with buzz saws.
And still I'm the pine-knot torch
carried by search parties
when you lose your child, the bed
carved of hard maple where you
breathe your last furry breath.

Two

Dysphoria: The Empress Dowager
Succumbs to Fox Lunacy

η *Empress Dowager Tzu-Hsi's limitless greed grew more and*
  more corrupt until the Qing Dynasty lost its power.
                                                    —*Beijing*

η *In Asia, depression was what most often left women open*
  to fox possession.
                                          —Chinese folk tale

She sneaks in, holding her tail high, skulking
about the palace, the two-hearted bitch.
Chinese foxes can become human in their 50th year.
That's enough of an opening for her.

She surveys her gardens through tight windows shaped
like fans, peaches: the costly boat cut from marble
that doesn't float, white hulk veined with boreal blue
haunting the lake, the knobby knees of cypress,

manmade rocks. *The Pavilion for Listening*
to Orioles Sing is where she drags herself, drowning
in opium and silk. *Rest.* Birds ridicule her and she turns
inside, trailing ponderous robes. Addicted

to opera: performance counts. Not quite mastering
the human form, she forbids mirrors which expose
her yellow eyes, a twitching whisker. She grows
more wanton; a painting of a waterfall gets nailed

31

above her bed. At night she hallucinates marriage,
carries pink lotus blossoms to her love, roots dripping
on her fragrant center. Her favorite number is six: six
eunuchs, six carved thrones, six Pekinese. No cats.

A fox who doesn't learn to trot beneath the moon
ends up building her nest inside your tomb, paws touching
the ebony boxes jammed full of everyday jewelry.
She hides your liver in her flowing sleeves.

When her greed demands that she be fed
a daily feast prepared by those who cannot love
her, her delicate jade cup and golden chopsticks
do not serve her well, do not disguise the maggots

left to flourish at her long table. Fever,
her head aches and thrums. Nothing helps: the tea
she takes, the smokes. The night smells of jasmine, clove
and urine. Peasants will die. She screams
because stirring the water still fails to make it clear.

Ringmaster

Every eye in the house is on you
unless the view is blocked by the fool

hawking peanuts, popcorn. The story
unfolding in the Big Tent gives you

a certain power. Your jodhpurs
ride tight on your thighs and I can tell

you've tried some cheap trick
with paint or shoe black to make them look

like leather. A whip pulses in your left hand, splays
sawdust at your feet. Suddenly you want

to crack a few backs open; you want slaves.
The most gifted overseers learned how

to land the lash in the same stripe
time and again, kissing muscle, then tendon,

fascia at last, before biting bone.
You are not a master, but a talent

nonetheless. Erratic attack, we don't know
when you'll demand we perform.

Trotting, gray flanks darkening, in a circle
or dangling from our knees, the lurid

trapeze not ever obliged to follow
its expected arc. Our costumes pinch.

People in the front row can see windows of flesh
through torn seams; rotten threads spew

sequins as we dance. I have never loved a circus,
Ringmaster. It's both contrived and dangerous:

one spark on canvas waterproofed with gas,
a mis-step from high wire, stampeding elephants.

A tawdry scene. It's hard finding myself here, mangy
as the muzzled bear led into the ring by men

down on their luck, tired as the tiger who
no longer knows anything but cage.

Look at the clown leaning beside the exit—blood-
colored lips, black crosses drawn through his eyes.

The Hourglass Heart

A seed or tear (pronounced to rhyme with "pear")
is what glass makers call an air bubble locked
in a finished piece of glass. This is an imperfection.
                    —Glass, Paper and Beans

everyone made such a fuss
as if it weren't possible
as if its womanly shape were somehow to blame

they acted like the hand-blown glass
riddled with seeds and tears
was too delicate to wring blood

two chambers are more than enough
holding   releasing
funneling the sadness of children, the silence
of living rooms   cupping love
long enough to heat it

I say   *here at last is a heart*
with clarity   a surgeon might
pause, might stroke its side
with a damp finger   this heart
sings in various pitches
depending how empty she is

Why Counting Sheep
Doesn't Work for Mothers

Lambs are born trying to die.

Sheep lead each other into the bawling creek,
roll onto their backs and bloat up, bleating
and helpless, worthless as wool. Sheep
invented *the grass is always greener,* wedge
heads into fence slats to prove it. Count
the number of ways they find to die: staggers
and braxy, pasturella. Blue tongue and scab,
blowfly strike. In the winter, it's hypothermia,
in summer, maggots and foxes, dogs and crows.
Sheep gorge and poison themselves on ragwort,
fallen ash leaves, timothy. They get depressed.
They graze all night in my bed of twisted linens.
In the glaze of dawn you are lost. The bell
around your neck is silent, strangled with ice.

Water Pressure

When we bought the house we had water pressure.
   The children were babies. With our first house we fell
      in love; we'd signed papers before we noticed there was no

fireplace. We were smarter now. We were parents.
   We turned on the faucets and flushed the johns. Water,
      generous and gushing, rinsed shampoo from the girls'

shiny hair. My husband brought it to me in a sparkling crystal glass,
   or he brought me a thirsty flower. Sometimes the pipes
      hummed and vibrated. Sometimes a faint pinging sound.

The water came on demand. It got harder. The girls pounded
   the wall when showering, if down below we washed sheets
      or dishes, if we flushed a toilet. They needed more water,

the supply dwindled. A surgeon said remove the pipes, install
   fresh white ones. But soon the children will be gone.
      My husband and I can shower together. We are not reduced.

Beyond the bedroom wall we will reminisce about water,
   how it flowed so freely and in such abundance. How we let it run
      over our open palms and through our fingers.

Marriage

Who breaks the thread—the one who pulls,
or the one who holds on?

The marriage depended on the yellow dog living.
  On seeing a daughter's fat red jacket moving

through the snow toward home. It relied on his knowing
  where Lake County was when she asked, not offering

answers that, to her, indicated a certain dullness:
  "not exactly." The marriage rested on small things

collected in a reliable fashion; leaves
  before snow, recyclables a day late following

holidays. At other times, it required more: him
  worrying about money, drawing up budgets that left

no room for a dead battery and towing, a broken window,
  a red coat. Required a rowboat full to the gunwales with bright fish

as they pull heavily toward shore, a wild finch outside the pane,
  stitching up the yellow morning while they eat toast.

You hear stories that don't surprise you. The woman
  whose husband gave her 18 red roses, *for the good years,*

on their 25th anniversary. The one who believed
  that by now she'd be clipping her husband's toenails, his thin

white leg resting extended across her lap. Instead she's tooling
  around Chicago with a lover young enough to be her son.

Consider the upkeep on anything you own. The effort
    involved over years to keep your roof from leaking,

to remove stains from holiday table linens. Honor the rhythm
    of repair: hammer to shingle, dishrag on plate, brushstroke

against dull wall. The iron pressed over a blue chambray shirt.
    Pleasing her can be like threading the tight, hard eye of a needle.

You, the thread, bend first too far right, too far left.
    You trim a sharper point, turn the needle so the larger

opening faces you, spit on the thread. Getting it right
    demands both vigilance and skill. Luck.

How do you know when your longing to move to Raleigh—
    or just west of town, where the view of sun-fall

is unobstructed except for pine boughs—is a true hunger,
    and when it's your recurring search for a geographical cure?

The image of a teeter-totter keeps showing up
    but it's not really that even-steven balance. Not

like balancing a budget. One person or the other
    is always scootching forward or back

on the splintery plank. A trusted partner might back off
    the low end, leaving the other to crash to the ground.

It happened to me once; my ankles folded and were trapped
    beneath the weight; the screw drove straight for the bone.

Mercury

A thermometer has broken in our junk drawer.
Daughters inform me that in Chemistry class,
it's like a death when mercury is on the loose.
Students are warned that if it goes down the drain
it will contaminate the world. Mercury is more

poisonous than lead or arsenic, I learn; the vapor
has no smell or taste, can't be detected
by human senses. It destroys brain
and kidney tissue in studies, is a known cause
of birth defects, schizophrenia and abnormal hunger.

If you touch it you may die from ALS,
Chronic Fatigue Syndrome, Crohn's Disease or madness.
I behave responsibly, e-mail my two best resources. Susan
tells me *wad it into a paper towel and toss it,*
cautions me not to lick the drawer; I'll be fine.

But my brother recalls a time 30 years ago,
when we captured spilled quicksilver in a Tupperware cup,
played with it for months while talking on the phone
or watching Mom make salad. This explains so much, I think.
Delayed puberty, beagles who baffled us by dying

one after another, my inability to do math or make puns. And later,
the addictions, compulsions, panic disorders? The pain
which shoots into my forehead during rainstorms in August,
the slapping of innocent children, my tears while driving past
cast-off tractors, combines. And so, I do nothing, don't open the draw

I imagine ponderous silver beads dividing and multiplying
among things we don't need but can't part with—snapshots
of family and friends with demon-red retinas, a screwdriver
with multiple heads, now rusty, my husband's gift for being best
man, those batteries we know are neither charged nor dead.

Water: Catalogue For An Exhibition

Starfish

A woman floats,
aerial perspective.
Face, toes, fingertips, breasts
breaking the surface.

Swimming Pool Without Mercy

The focus here is on the filter
which skims the surface—
what it takes from water.
A vole, wasps, a band-aid,
a hummingbird, iridescent
Japanese beetles strung like jewelry
on the single hair of a young girl.

Overflow

A black two-piece bathing suit
floats like an angelfish in the sink.
The washbowl is plugged; water
spills generously over the sides
onto the tiles. The bar of soap, the wooden
hairbrush, a blue box of tampons.

Pyrite

Off the coast of Coronado, a woman wades
for miles, treading through glitter,
yielding a wake of suspended gold.

Setting Sail

A tall ship, mast
and rigging. The sails are women
in white voile. Their arms extend
weightlessly toward each other.
Wind fills their skirts.

The Movement of Water

The water, its ripples and planes, its spackling
of light on dark. The question of how
blue sky reflects below as green.

The Other Shoe

It's a commanding shoe, satin spike, black, sharp
as the stakes holding a burning circus tent in place. Not
the red Capezios with floppy flowers she slips into beside the pool.

Not the brocade slippers of 12th-century noblemen,
elongated toes curling so high they employed fine chains
and ribbons to steer their steps. A marionette of self.

Maybe we're counting clouds or age spots on our arms, zebra
mussels fused to the rusted coffee can beneath the dock.
Maybe we're counting the length of intervals between one lawnmower

stopping and another beginning, thinking about the times
his hand grazed but didn't quite connect with that irresistible place,
ways to say *dapple* without using that word.

Say it drops on Kyaiktiyo, the Buddhist pagoda teetering on a precipice
and the whole world shifts. Families sweeping the shaded path clean
of leaves as darkness lifts, holy bells in the distance.

Woman of Water

You were wise, clinging
to the shore, the side
of the lost vessel. You
should be afraid. Oh sure,
I douse barn fires,
passed in buckets
from neighbor to
neighbor as they stand
in their foolish nightshirts.
I'll sweeten the dirt
of your June garden.
But I'm moody,
move from trickle
to gush in the time it takes
a tear, a needle
of rain, to drop.
Ask the fishermen
who've encountered me
off Newfoundland
in November, when
I'm so lush with plankton
that I swallow the light,
when my rogue waves
are mistaken for the moon.

Three

Windshield

I extend, stretch out and pull the blade
hard across the windshield, wash the glass clear
again. Gone, the tiny smears of bugs who overpaid
to fly, bird droppings, sap from the pine tree near
where I park. This Shell station is on the way,
and we're waiting for the tank to fill. Inside
the car, my daughter stares; she doesn't say
what she sees dead ahead of her. She might have died
that night although we don't speak of it. She's begun
a higher dose today, stronger medicine to bring
her back to herself, back to all of us stunned
to find her so still. The side-effects she swallows sting
my eyes, the glass between us now clear and black.
We're on this road together. I want her back.

The Tenth Muse

Euphoria showed up
in cowboy drag, the smell
of cedar everywhere.
In six months
I will open the linen closet
for a pillowcase
and its whisper
will bring me to my knees.

February was too warm, unnatural. Euphoria wore three pairs
of pants for protection. She was skinny. Her mask was my daughter's
face. She didn't look healthy but beautiful: dark curls out of control,
high color in her cheeks, black eyes that glittered and threw sparks.

She packed light.
Her horseshoe was as rusty
as her gun. A whip.
Red satin, an address
and a piece of lapis.
She'd been ambushed
trying to get out of Dodge.

Euphoria had a lot to learn.
Train schedules and basic safety
rules. The gaps in her world
history the size of a large ranch. She ran
water and took constant baths, told us
water transforms one emotion into another.

After Euphoria had spun in her saddle for three days and three nights
they corralled her.

It's hard
not to like her.
She's funny
asking the doctor
for marijuana, cow poking
his questions:

Who do you believe I am?
. . . the Emperor?
We don't have Emperors in America, he says.

Euphoria is not afraid to look crazy.

Euphoria buzzes, a mass
of African bees, a pack of jackals.
No animal
you can turn
your back on.

Euphoria wakes up
exhausted
from her adventure.
Her heart is broken.
We did not win the war.
World hunger still happening.
She did not even climb
to the top of the mountain
although she came close.
People say she is sick.
Poor Euphoria.

51

My daughter has a friend with a brain disease.
They play tennis each night in the dark.
They eat paint chips and nutritional yeast,
reminisce about when they could drink beer.
It is clear that one of them will die first.

Tell me what I was like in the hospital, Mom.
You looked so sad. I only stayed there because of your face.

What is clear is that Euphoria grew up
around water. And she was not my daughter's friend.
In fact, I'd have to say we were not acquainted.
If she has splashed in our pool, skinny-dipping
after the family has gone to bed, after the father
had locked the doors and believed everyone safe,
we didn't know.

> *I imagine the two of them*
> *sitting in a garden*
> *among late-blooming roses*
> *and dark cascades of leaves,*
> *letting the landscape speak for them*
> *leaving us nothing to overhear.*
>
> —Lisel Mueller

They say people make love after bouts of loss and death.

If I ask my husband what he remembers, he says the sun
when we stepped into the hospital parking lot.
Walking our dog when we got home.

It doesn't help that this is the illness
of Emily Dickinson, Cole Porter &
Vincent Van Gogh. It is also the illness
of Theresia who lives behind Dairy Queen
and Nancy who weighs 300 pounds from her meds.
I don't want to talk about my work.

Pick a noun, any noun.
Write it on the paper (down)
You could rhyme o girl o mine

but you can't sleep.

The mind is agile: onion rings, Lord of the Rings,
for whom the bell rings, and then
The car we're in is just a memory. The real car is in the garage.

Of course, no one has traction all the time.

My daughter is back, cuts
Martha Stewart's face
from the front of *Time,*
mounts it, and glues it on a stick.
She creates a Martha mask and pops
into doorways wearing it.
Her sisters scream like someone
is pulling their legs under water.

In the hospital she built an altar on the radiator.
What can we bring for it, we ask?
Dirt, she says. *Air.*

Deciding

While you were deciding
   whether you wanted to keep on

living last spring, I was in Amsterdam,
   trying to figure out how de Heem

decided to let the lemon peel
   dangle off the edge of the table,

its pocked curl growing brown,
   while two pears sat untouched.

Entering the conversation seemed
   for you to be like the Double Dutch I played

in my safe neighborhood as a girl, revolving
   rope ends hooked through a stationary eye

screwed to Smythe's garage. The rhythm
   clicked smooth and regular. I heard it

in my head: *now go, now, now, now*
   but the arch and circle—the mystery

of non-intersection, right hand turning
   then left—kept me just off balance, hypnotized.

While you were trying to decide whether to jump
   in or not, I was drinking chardonnay, or, tell

the truth, Amstel sold in vending
   machines for two euros. I kept returning

to art, straining to see what Peeters and Beert chose
   to reveal, where they held back. And sometimes

you'd enter the picture, asleep in that pink,
   girlish bedroom, sisters beside you,

and sometimes your lonely father, driving
   you from one small town to another.

Carvings

Certain happenings . . . leave indelible and distressing memories—
memories to which the sufferer continually returns, and by which
he is tormented by day and by night
                                        —Pierre Janet

In the aftermath, my spine was a totem pole carved
image by hard image, layered like the clothes
you refused to peel off in the hospital that night—

leggings, then jeans, chaps and old ski pants
with spiders on the cuffs. I remember thinking *Spider*
Sabitch shot with his own Luger. You were thin,

we could count the rings on your spine (on your fingers,
your toes—nobody knows). These are not nicks
in my heart muscle, not faint notches in a cage

of ribs, keeping score. These carvings click
against each other in the night like beads on an abacus,
elaborate, arbitrary, particular. This odd temple of memory

impressed etching by etching, God's heft leaning
into the bezel, and still, the smell something that might come
from a novice's wood-burning kit. The artist exerted force

here, burned a diorama of battle into a plum pit. This sailor mad
for shore sharpened his sail needle and scratched out a woman
on whale's tooth, darkened her nipples with squid ink.

Scoliosis of memory, I want you gone. Translate yourself
into story, and I'll consent to live with the crooked spine, its bend
and weight. But for now I'm grabbing the chisel, cutting bantams

fighting on the bellies of dried gourds, etching embryos
like pink shrimp into ice, into egg shells. Bring me antlers
shed in a February meadow—I'll show you carving.

Drifts

You imagine it will end sometime, the way your father
talked about left turns, how there's always an opening
if you wait long enough. It can't go on forever, snow
falling through the sifter, smothering the world. Still,
in the back room of your mind, a story, Ray Bradbury
maybe, where the snow did not stop. The people believed
it would. Believed they'd drop shirts at the dry cleaners
the next morning, buy eggs at the corner store.
But it crept up past window sills, interred gardens,
shrubbery. The yellow plows and salt wagons were buried
alive. I remember it as a quiet violence: how it first blocked out sound
and finally light, how it choked eaves and plugged the chimney.
Sometimes I think it will be like that, drifts of loss, whole hills
of sorrow, me with no shovel, no strong back to tunnel out.

Any God

The rocks beneath her heart began to move
the night her daughter lost her native tongue.
No god of French-milled soap and lavender
could build a church on cradled hands and love.

The night that artist lost her native tongue
something seismic dropped, rolled away,
faith in that childish church of hands tested
and sung, the green-faced violinist played.

Something seismic drops through an open heart
these nights, gone missing between the cradle and now.
The face of the violinist green and dark,
fiddling toward some unknown gift, not found.

Gone missing between the cradle and now, hands reach
for any god—of hardboiled eggs, of nail heads—
fiddling on toward gifts not recognized nor found.
The girl keeps playing, beating time. She says

any god will do: god of plum pits, ice cubes,
dog hair, there's always something to believe in.
This girl—the gift we recognize—found
and rocked, o hourglass god, beneath my heart.

Lapidary

We might find the rough stones anywhere, smoke
or rose quartz near Whitefish Bay, fire agate
in Arizona. For you, it was bloodstone
on the floor of a Chicago subway, getting

slapped around, then eight days on a psych ward.
We hold it up to the light, concentrating
on the image beneath its raw surface:
the smell, not exactly like something burning,

the language you played like Crack the Whip.
In the weeks when we didn't know
if you would kill yourself, I'd go down
to the basement, put on the tight loupe that carved

red marks on my forehead. I needed to see
this differently, find a way to recognize the irregular
patterns in the formation, chalcedony of memory.
We worked to turn it into story, cobbing

it, hammering with the lightest touch, knocking
off the brittle bits: what we knew about drug use, you
bumming money in the train station, carrying a bottle
of red wine, carrying a whip. We need to smooth this

into a diagnosis we can all live with. We dump these stones
into the tumbling barrel, add strong abrasives. Water and grit
begin their slow work, days, weeks, months. We can still
hear them falling like the bottom might drop out.

In the end, we will need a diamond bit, a grindstone
harder than the stone itself to cut and polish
this story into the shape we ache for—your sweet face a cameo.
We'll cut it from tiger's eye. I'll wear it around my neck.

Sorrow

You see her at the bar in her rent-to-own gown, fingers
grasping her matching plastic purse. Her lips are chapped, eyes
rimmed red. She's been waiting for you to marry her.

You're no virgin, have slept with sadness, slow-danced
with grief. But something about this set-up makes
you balk. You know she'd be a jealous bride, wouldn't let you

out of her sight, would keep you mowing the lawn, sneaking out to p
cards. Marrying her would mean sleeping under an old army blanket
half-warm and pinned down, unable to move your legs in the night.

Of course, she has her charms. Her teeth are white and even. You g
way back, remember her when she had the biggest breasts,
full lips. She used to wash her face with French milled soap

shaped like a hen with three eggs. She's let herself go.
You slide onto the stool beside her, avoid her eyes,
drink whatever she's not having.

The Powerlessness of Ghosts

Ghosts can't travel across open water.
They don't show up in photo albums like girls
with pale skin and perfect eyebrows. They
can't drive cars with stick shifts because
of the clutch, aren't good spellers, can't
eat rice with chopsticks. They don't watch
re-runs of *Ren and Stimpy*, don't know
about forgiveness. You don't expect much
from ghosts: they're not interested in art
or revolution or healing, won't threaten
to run off to Los Angeles and become famous.
They are lousy at managing money.
Ghosts are mostly good at self defense.
A few stay in shape, can kickbox high
as your heart, study anatomy, know which
pressure points deliver blue-ribbon pain.

Woman of Garlic

In trade I'm nothing.
A pound of ground ginger
root could buy a sheep;
the same weight of nutmeg,
seven cows. Cinnamon
brought its weight in gold,
and a sack of pepper—
priceless, peppercorn
after peppercorn changing
hands to settle men's debts.
One clove alters a whole dish,
improves the taste of meat
gone bad. One bulb makes soldiers
brave in battle, cures 61 diseases.
I serve modestly, paper
dress hiding many bodies,
healing or embalming.

Four

Vulpes Vulpes

O graceful carnivore, it's not your cunning
I admire, considering you in my yard, knees
weak as I witness the apparent ease
with which you adapt to anything, running
wild over golf courses, the cemetery just uphill
from where I watch. Not exactly a surprise,
your foxiness, after all, your yellow eyes
take in everything—born blind, soon you will
hear mice squeal two fields away, see us, fools
who strain to make peace with change. Our window
frames voles, wrens, sunflower seeds—some slow mouse
becoming dinner, and you, prince among the toadstools,
high-rises, grasses, outfoxing the entire show,
relaxed, elegant even, making the unfamiliar home.

Loosestrife

She knows the symptoms of healing may not
be obvious to a new practitioner,
may not present like leprosy, missionaries

touching stove burners, not feeling
their flesh sear until they smell it.
The signs might masquerade

as further disease: heart penetrated
by a toxic dose of honeysuckle
or mock orange—fragrance, the toughest

stem of memory. Or as a cramp that throws
you down on the bed, sobbing
into a pile of just-folded laundry.

The mechanics of healing may resemble
a pioneering eye surgery before they've refined it.
The kind that restores your vision to a burlesque

of normal, makes you almost able to see
that the child you're swimming after is your son.
She knows you might feel you're losing

ground, a bear riding the subway in Piscataway. Yet
she believes she can collect the antidote, believes
she has it in her. She will drive a white convertible, arm extended

casually through the open window like she's drying
her nails. She skirts the cities, heads instead for wilderness
campgrounds, the steady fathers smoking pipes

in outhouses to disguise the smell. She sets shoeboxes
at the bases of trees, the far ends of tunnels, harvests
loosestrife, purple carpets rolled down aisles

on either side of the river. In August, when the bats return,
she hunts the shadows of bonfires on west-facing lakes,
gathers enough of what she needs.

Drifting down the Manistee and Pigeon in tractor tubes,
she wears wool socks, keeping heat where it belongs
even when wet, seeks the deep spots where soothing trout pool.

Retreat

The experienced retreatant brings a change
of underwear, one thin book. I bring 16 books, a boom box,
22 CDs, 2 bottles of wine, 3 grocery sacks: quinoa, acorn
squash, shaggy-headed mushrooms and shriveled grapefruit.
I bring my own Buddha chair, my own pillow, fork,
Tampax, fire logs. I bring boxes of Firechief kitchen matches,

and a fire extinguisher, each in its own deerskin pouch.
I bring a silver cigarette case engraved
with the name of the girl I stole it from 25 years ago.
I bring the wet filament stretching from the tongue
to the roof of the fat lady's mouth, salt, spit, no sound found
in nature. I bring slivered almonds that remind me

of torn fingernails. Banana slices I know to be the dark-
eyed faces of babies drowning in mother's milk. Inside
my extra hiking boots, 10 lbs of bird seed which I'll scatter
to rot on the windowsill. I bring blood clots the size
of small canaries, ribbons of slush pelting the windshields
of those who try to rescue me. I bring a lonely broom

contrived of reeds and sage smudge which will never sweep
my cabin clean again. Shiny globes of chicken fat in red
and white cans which I tease out with a hemostat and rub
beneath my eyes. I bring a bird whose song I've never heard
and place him in a tree outside the bathroom window,
words I can't find in the thesaurus or dictionary.

I bring fringed blankets and weary shawls, all wool, all blue.
I bring socks of each color which I hang from hooks and doorknobs
like surrender flags. Tarot cards, wicker baskets, venison cooked
in rosemary by my grandmother, a beat-up fedora. I bring doors, sor
left half-open for me to run into in the belly of the night, some that I
to unheated rooms, some which refuse to open at all.

The memory of barns. Handfuls of vitamins E, C and B Complex,
Calcium. Primrose oil which I take last because it's what I need
the most. I cast the footprints of raccoons onto the surface
of the frozen pond, reminding myself not to walk a straight path
across ice. I bring a book on birds, but no birds. A platter full of stars,
three dolls named Pilfer, Plunder and Forage, a rice bowl of tears.

What Supports Life

Two deer leave their beds unmade
in the deep grass, chew away the edges
of mist in front of my cabin. Nine
wild turkeys. Yesterday, a red-backed
salamander serene in stump-rot.
My first bluebird, twice.

Nature is so cocky, so sure of itself.
The wind moves from ridge to ridge
like some contagious disease.
My daughter tracks mud
onto the wool rug, gunning off
in my white car.

A nuthatch struts straight down
the maple. Trees. You know how
they are. Standing there like
they own the place. It makes me want
to push them around. Look
for the leafless ones with no roots.

Back in my cabin, I read that one snag
can support life for 50 years. And birds.
Always positioning for power: either *look-at-me*
perches, the kingbird on a dead stalk,
or concealing themselves entirely behind leaves,
forcing me to look straight up into the sun.

It's not like I know nothing
about nature. How to recognize
a blue racer, yellow jacket from bumblebee,
sumac when it isn't fall. I know ladybugs
avoid Lake Michigan on gusty days,
their wings that fragile.

The downy woodpecker's tongue,
too long to store in his mouth, begins
in a nostril and curls over his skull
before extruding from bottom beak.
My daughter has added a hole
and surgical steel ornament

to her perfect tongue. She sleeps
in a barn, has a cat and 9 gay men
to keep her company. I read
that the Japanese leash cormorants
like hunting dogs to fish for them;
the collar keeps them from swallowing.

My daughter is sketching, slender fingers
firmly wrapped around charcoal. Or searing
radicchio with garlic, asking too late
if I like the bitter taste. I carry a white
porcelain bowl of tears and a small tuft
of rabbit fur to the creek bed.

Like the white campion that paves my path
this morning, she blooms at night, for all I know
is pollinated by moths. I cross a field
of mown timothy; a butterfly lights on my shoelace,
orange, the way roof tiles in Florence
or Crete vibrate against sky, its blue thorax.

Sun in her hair when I used to wash
it in the lake, before it coiled
around her face like a nest
of green snakes. I've grown serious
about birdcalls, wildflowers recently,
pay more attention to what supports life.

I look for the difference between simple
and compound leaves, between annual
and perennial, want so badly
to believe the story that, beneath
the down, the nest of the baby eagle
has as its bottom layer, thorn.

Woman of Paper

Invented by wasps
who chew decayed wood
then spit, for centuries
my messages were carried
on the bark and leaves of trees, the skin
of young goats. Next, rags: our babies' diapers,
napless sheets, the torn shirts of our men,
our petticoats, our hankies.
When we had given everything
we had, forbidden to bury our dead
in cotton or linen, they sent to Egypt
for mummies, added water lilies, turnips,
sugarcane and dust to the mess.
The day they noticed *Vespidae* laborers,
it all shifted to lumberjacks,
gamy giants with black beards
who slept in enormous bunks,
spit and spun stories
by the light of oil lanterns.
After that, I was easier
to come by, had a higher acid content.
Never again so durable.
Never again so fine.

Beckon Road

I've heard lots of names
for those type clouds
            fish scale
            mares' tails
            chicken scratchings
the high thin ones
that don't reflect in a lake.

                *

Got up as far as Michigan
once. Those trees
was so full of bings
they looked red. We ate
them by the fistful.
At the end of the day
you knew the water
at the pump would be pure ice.

                *

I used to be real hardy
and quick as a finger snap.
Steady on a ladder too,
a good one for tree work.
Mostly now all's I eat
is cereal. Lester says
I'm just knobs and gullies.
All leaking away.

                *

In the dream
the water is moving,
fast but not so cold.

I'm holding Ellen's hand
and she says, "Billy,
your legs got no meat."

*

Granddaddy
used to walk with me.
We'd pick up stones
and arrange them under a tree.
When it was time
to hit the road, he'd grin,
say, "Leave 'em be, boy.
Let 'em grow up into big stones."

*

Tomatoes in Arkansas.
That was hot. Your own
sweat made you feel bugs
was dancing on your back.
Sometimes lunch was potato peels
in a hanky. Sometimes lard
spread thin on bread, sweet dark tea.

*

My momma used to set
flowers in a jar. So I picked
some for Ellen once
and she said, "Sweet
Jesus, Billy, ain't I seen
enough wild carrot
in this world? Go
bring me a co-cola."

*

That lake, now that
was a humbling thing.
Ellen was the only
one went in regular.
That woman could
float for hours
and not turn blue.

*

"Make friends with dust,"
I used to tell Lester. "It'll pile
up on your teeth and make your tears
and sweat run brown."
Baseball game in Lone Grove,
Oklahoma once. I slid
into home and that dust tail
was so high and thick
no one could say
if I was safe or out.

*

In the dream
I buy Ernie Pratt's pick-up.
I drive off and look real proud,
then I see he sold it mean
cause the truck bed
is full of cat bones.

*

When the baby died
she just cleared out.
Left a sorry pile
in the house down back
where we was living.
Set the booties momma
knit her right on the top.
That hurt momma bad
but I knew she left
them there for me.

*

Coda:

Ellen says, *Billy had more dreams*
than pitches in a road.
Carried a mayonnaise jar full
of white sand, fine as salt, as long
as I knew him. Wanted a place
on Beckon Road, where
that bay was "blue as cornflowers."
What kind of man talks like that?

Sweeping at the End of Summer

She's steady, moves her broom down the narrow path,
left to right, left, right. The long pine cones,
sappy and unopened, stain the concrete.

She thinks of her mother, her grandmother.
There are no neighbor children bickering,
no dogs or birds, just the sweeping.

A noise so repetitive feels like silence.
Not like the return of yellow jackets or crickets.
More like light suddenly falling short

of the window where she's seen it
each morning all summer, a branch
of dogwood turning scarlet overnight.

Watching the Lake Freeze Over

Watching the lake freeze over
is almost a fifth season.
Those who know it are unmoved, blasé,
but I walk down to the shore needing
to understand how one thing becomes another.
How even what seems precipitate
occurs over time. In deep water,
the waves are still forming a heady line,
but closer to home they slow up—
like an old 45 on the wrong speed,
voices flattening out and deepening.
At my feet, exactly where the dock stands
in summer, the lake grows gelatinous,
thickening and setting, the time
right to slice in the banana. Even
the geese are fooled. Coming in
to land on what poses as open water,
their tail feathers leave fat skidmarks on new ice.
Conversely, the day you think you can walk
across this ice to freedom and new loneliness,
a lapping sound close to shore—
mallards beginning to turn
upside down in this water, feeding
on whatever persists there.

Envoi

What Happened Then

And when it is almost dark, Susan
calls, *come outside and lie down*
and I do and look up and the sky
is stippled with dragonflies
shooting the rapids of air currents, darting
and bobbing up by the chimney.
A feeding, we suppose, hopefully
mosquitoes. *How many*, I wonder out loud
and Susan says, after a moment, *thirty-five*.

photo by Victoria Reichow

Gail Martin, a Michigan native, grew up in Flint. She earned a B.A. from Kalamazoo College and recently completed her Master's degree in clinical social work. Her work has appeared in numerous literary magazines, including *Rattle*, *Primavera*, *Poetry Northwest* and *Folio*. Martin was selected by Alice Fulton as the 1999 Winner of the National Poet Hunt sponsored by *The MacGuffin*. She lives with her husband and three left-handed daughters in Kalamazoo, Michigan.

New Issues Poetry & Prose

Editor, Herbert Scott

Vito Aiuto, *Self-Portrait as Jerry Quarry*
James Armstrong, *Monument In A Summer Hat*
Claire Bateman, *Clumsy*
Michael Burkard, *Pennsylvania Collection Agency*
Christopher Bursk, *Ovid at Fifteen*
Anthony Butts, *Fifth Season*
Anthony Butts, *Little Low Heaven*
Kevin Cantwell, *Something Black in the Green Part of Your Eye*
Gladys Cardiff, *A Bare Unpainted Table*
Kevin Clark, *In the Evening of No Warning*
Cynie Cory, *American Girl*
Jim Daniels, *Night with Drive-By Shooting Stars*
Joseph Featherstone, *Brace's Cove*
Lisa Fishman, *The Deep Heart's Core Is a Suitcase*
Robert Grunst, *The Smallest Bird in North America*
Paul Guest, *The Resurrection of the Body and the Ruin of the World*
Robert Haight, *Emergences and Spinner Falls*
Mark Halperin, *Time as Distance*
Myronn Hardy, *Approaching the Center*
Brian Henry, *Graft*
Edward Haworth Hoeppner, *Rain Through High Windows*
Cynthia Hogue, *Flux*
Janet Kauffman, *Rot* (fiction)
Josie Kearns, *New Numbers*
Maurice Kilwein Guevara, *Autobiography of So-and-so: Poems in Prose*
Ruth Ellen Kocher, *When the Moon Knows You're Wandering*
Ruth Ellen Kocher, *One Girl Babylon*
Steve Langan, *Freezing*
Lance Larsen, *Erasable Walls*
David Dodd Lee, *Downsides of Fish Culture*
Deanne Lundin, *The Ginseng Hunter's Notebook*
Joy Manesiotis, *They Sing to Her Bones*

Sarah Mangold, *Household Mechanics*
Gail Martin, *The Hourglass Heart*
David Marlatt, *A Hog Slaughtering Woman*
Gretchen Mattox, *Goodnight Architecture*
Paula McLain, *Less of Her*
Sarah Messer, *Bandit Letters*
Malena Mörling, *Ocean Avenue*
Julie Moulds, *The Woman with a Cubed Head*
Gerald Murnane, *The Plains* (fiction)
Marsha de la O, *Black Hope*
C. Mikal Oness, *Water Becomes Bone*
Elizabeth Powell, *The Republic of Self*
Margaret Rabb, *Granite Dives*
Rebecca Reynolds, *Daughter of the Hangnail; The Bovine Two-Step*
Martha Rhodes, *Perfect Disappearance*
Beth Roberts, *Brief Moral History in Blue*
John Rybicki, *Traveling at High Speeds* (enlarged second edition)
Mary Ann Samyn, *Inside the Yellow Dress*
Ever Saskya, *The Porch is a Journey Different From the House*
Mark Scott, *Tactile Values*
Martha Serpas, *Côte Blanche*
Diane Seuss-Brakeman, *It Blows You Hollow*
Elaine Sexton, *Sleuth*
Marc Sheehan, *Greatest Hits*
Sarah Jane Smith, *No Thanks—and Other Stories* (fiction)
Phillip Sterling, *Mutual Shores*
Angela Sorby, *Distance Learning*
Russell Thorburn, *Approximate Desire*
Rodney Torreson, *A Breathable Light*
Robert VanderMolen, *Breath*
Martin Walls, *Small Human Detail in Care of National Trust*
Patricia Jabbeh Wesley, *Before the Palm Could Bloom: Poems of Africa*